CRUISING

A view through the porthole

More than you ever wanted to know
about taking a cruise!

LEE H. VAN DAM

LHVD *Books!*
Lee H. Van Dam

CRUISING A view through the porthole

Copyright © 2014 by Lee H. Van Dam, All Rights Reserved

All art by Emily E. Ferguson
Copyright © 2014 by Lee H. Van Dam

Book design by Rebecca Hayes
www.beckypublisher.com

Published in the United States by
LHVD Books
Sandy, Utah
www.lhvdbooks.com

ISBN: 978-0-9903610-0-8

Library of Congress Control Number 2014908586

Contents

1. What Floats Your Boat? 1
2. How Far Away Is the Horizon? 5
3. A Topsy-Turvy Stomach and a Strange and Giddy Head 9
4. Are Weddings Performed by Ship Captains Legal? 13
5. Bow Thrusters – How Do You Parallel Park a Cruise Ship? 17
6. I Spy… a Lighthouse 21
7. A Sanitation Score of 96… What Does That Mean? 27
8. Eggs Benedict at the Panama Canal 31
9. What Is Pod Propulsion? 35
10. Smokestacks on the Titanic 39
11. Do You Remember Gopher, Your Yeoman Purser? 43
12. The "Ests" of Cruise Ships 47
13. One Crew Member's Employment Contract 51
14. Stretching the Ship – and the Revenue 57
15. How Are You at "Sending the Biscuit?" 61
16. Are Ships Still Christened? 65
17. What Is the Status of Fire Safety on Cruise Ships? 69
18. Turn Down That Rock-n-Roll! 75
19. A Light and Whistle on My Life Jacket? 79
20. Prefabricated Staterooms – Without Floors 83
21. A Stateroom Is Better Than a Cabin – Or Is It? 87
22. Ft. Lauderdale, We Have a Problem. A Good One! 91
23. The Road Less Traveled 95
24. I Love Teak Deck Chairs! 99
25. What About Cruise Ship Art Auctions? 103

About the Author 108

What Floats Your Boat?

Good morning, class. Welcome to **Physics 101** where today we will study how boats float. First, let's conduct an experiment. **We are going to see if a metal object will float.** For this experiment we will need the following:
- A body of water - I have filled the kitchen sink with water.
- A metal object - I have gotten out a 5-ounce can of tuna fish from the pantry.
- A can opener, a spoon, a glass of water, and a hammer - I have put all four items out on the counter by the sink.

Place the object (the unopened tuna fish can) in the body of water. **You will notice that it immediately sinks.** Now use the can opener to open the can and then spoon out all of the contents. Wash out the can so it is clean. Place the empty tuna fish can on top of the water. What does it do now? **It floats.** Now slowly pour some water into the tuna fish can. What is it doing now? It is floating, but it is sitting lower in the water than before. Keep adding water to the can. What happens? The can sits lower and lower in the water until it finally sinks. Now take it out of the water and flatten the can with the hammer. Place it on the water. What happens? **The flattened tuna fish can sinks.**

What have we learned from the experiment? **We have learned that metal objects, under certain conditions, can float!** And using scientific reasoning, we may infer that large boats made out of metal, under certain conditions, can also float. In simplified terms, **this is because any object will float when its density is less than the density of the fluid it is put into.** Archimedes (287 BC – 212 BC), the famous Greek physicist and mathematician, discovered this concept (as well as related principles about displacement, buoyancy, etc.) as he was taking a bath. Remember the story? Upon making his discovery, he was so excited that he jumped out of the tub and ran naked through the streets of Syracuse yelling "Eureka!" meaning "I have found it!" When we say the density of an object, **we mean the average density of the entire object taken as a whole,** not just the density of the outer surface or skin of the object.

Density is expressed as mass per unit of volume. Water has a density of about **62 pounds per cubic foot.** Seawater, which is a little bit denser than regular water, has a density of about **64 pounds per cubic foot.** We say "about" because the density of water changes with temperature. Warm water is less dense than cold water.

In terms of the tuna fish can, when it was unopened and full of tuna, its average density was greater than 62 pounds per cubic foot, so it sank. The can without the food floated because the average density of the object (the empty metal can and the air inside the can) was less than 62 pounds per foot. When we then took the air out of the can by flattening it, it sank because the density of the metal by itself was greater than 62 pounds per foot.

When we talk about the density of a large ship, **we mean the average density of the entire ship – the metal hull, the decks, the cabins, the passengers, the luggage, the cargo, the great quantities of food on board, and the air in the ship.** All of this added together makes for an object that is less dense on average than the water the ship is sailing in. **So it floats – just like the empty tuna fish can floated.** This, of course, is because a good portion of the interior volume of the ship is air which is significantly less dense than seawater. So in designing a ship, what engineers need to do to make it float is to shape the metal skin of the vessel (i.e. the hull) **wide enough, long enough, and deep enough** so that the interior of the ship will contain sufficient space and air to allow the ship to float.

Now let's think about some applications of this principle. **Why do life jackets keep people afloat?** Because with a life jacket on, a person's average density has been decreased and the object (the object in this case is the person and the life jacket) has a lower average density than water. **Why do helium balloons float in air?** Because the density of the balloon with helium in it makes the total object (the blown-up rubber balloon plus the helium) less dense on average than the surrounding air. **And why does Ivory Soap float?** Because during the manufacturing process they add air to the mixture as a machine whips up the soap's ingredients. The resulting bar of soap is less dense than water, so it floats.

An interesting part of the principle of flotation as it applies to cruising is that **you can build ships out of non-buoyant materials (such as aluminum, steel, or perhaps even concrete)** so long as you design them with enough interior volume so that their average density is less than the density of water. **Being less dense than water is what floats your boat.**

Thanks, class. Should we now have a test on the material?

Nautical Term

Pipe Down

To pipe down means to be quiet and to stop talking. On sailing ships, the **bosun** had the responsibility to give signals to the crew by blowing his bosun's pipe, a pipe that gave out a shrill whistle. (A bosun was sometimes called a boatswain. He was selected by the captain to help supervise the sailors up on deck.) At the end of each day the bosun would give the last piping signal of the day – **the pipe down signal**. This signal meant that it was time for those up on the deck who didn't have night duties **to go down below and to be quiet for the night.**

How Far Away Is the Horizon?

As my wife and I were having dinner with a group of friends on a recent cruise, an interesting conversation was taking place between two of the men at the table. In a rather heated manner they were offering their opinions on **how far away the horizon is from the ship**. One said that he was sure it was more than 15 miles away and the other felt the horizon was perhaps only five or six miles away.

So how far away is the horizon from a cruise ship -- and how might one go about calculating that distance?

Because of the curvature of the earth, the distance between you and the horizon when you look out over the ocean depends on your height above the surface of the water. **More precisely, the distance depends on the height of your eyes above the water.** The following diagram helps illustrate that the distance to the horizon varies depending on the height of the observer:

A formula for calculating the approximate distance is:

square root(height in feet/0.5736) = distance to the horizon in miles

For instance, if your eyes are five feet above the ocean, the distance is approximately three miles. If your eyes are 100 feet above the ocean, the distance to the horizon is around 13.2 miles.

In more practical terms, if you were on a **small yacht** or were looking out of a lower porthole on a big ship your eyes might be 10 feet above the water, so the horizon would be about **4.2 miles away.** But standing on the deck of a **medium-size cruise ship** your eyes might be 150 feet above the water, so the horizon would be approximately **16.2 miles away.** And if your eyes were level with the **top of the funnel** of the **Oasis of the Seas** (one of the largest cruise ships built) your eyes would be 236 feet above the water and the horizon would be approximately **20.3 miles away.**

So which of the two men at the dinner table was correct? They both could be. It all depends on where on the ship they choose to be when looking at the horizon.

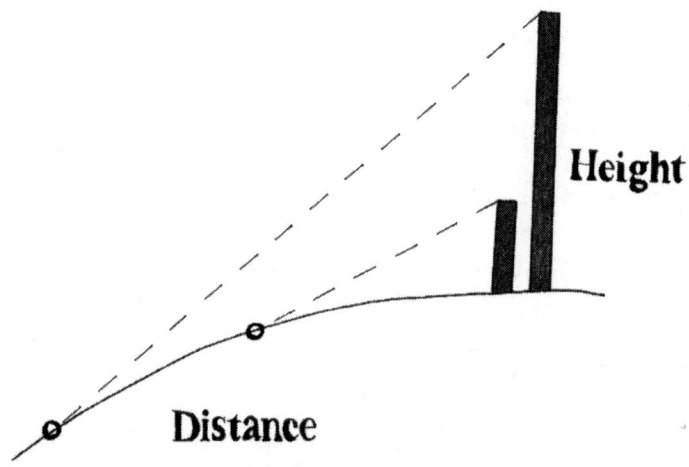

Nautical Term

Blubber

Blubber: As in "to weep loudly, like a child." When the sailors on whaling ships cooked and boiled the **blubber** or fat taken from the whales they caught, the fat would run down in large globules from the surface. So when sailors would see someone crying profusely, they would call it **blubbering**.

A Topsy-Turvy Stomach and a Strange and Giddy Head

In Herman Melville's novel, **Redburn: His First Voyage,** the main character, Wellingborough Redburn is traveling from New York to Liverpool on his first ocean voyage. When the ship gets out into open sea, Wellingborough experiences the following:

"I now began to feel unsettled and ill at ease about the stomach, as if matters were all topsy-turvy there; and felt strange and giddy about the head."

When the stomachs of passengers on cruise ships begin feeling **topsy-turvy** and their heads feel **strange and giddy**, what is the cause and what can be done about it?

Studies indicate that about **one-third** of cruise ship passengers are susceptible to some degree of seasickness, even if the sea is relatively calm. Under severe sea conditions, as many as **two-thirds** of the passengers will experience ill feelings. The seasickness happens because the motion of the ship creates a sensory conflict of information to the brain. The brain then responds by sending distress signals to other parts of the body, especially the nervous system and the stomach. All this can lead to dizziness, nausea, and vomiting.

Although there was not much that Wellingborough Redburn could do in 1849 to relieve his sea sickness, **today we are fortunate to have a number of remedies we can turn to.** How well they work varies from person to person and from situation to situation.

Over-the-counter pills are the least expensive and most common way to deal with seasickness. They are available in most drug and grocery stores, as well as on board the ship at the gift shop or from the purser's desk. For many people these pills work well, especially if taken before they begin feeling sick. A side effect of some pills is that they make you feel sleepy, so buying the non-drowsy version of the medication is something you might want to consider.

Another popular way to deal with seasickness is to use **a transdermal behind-the-ear patch**. These patches, which are only available through a prescription, provide a small continuous dosage of a drug called scopolamine. Each patch lasts for three days. More expensive than over-the-counter medications, the cost of the patches is covered by many health insurance plans.

For many people, **wrist bands** are another interesting choice. On the inside of each of your wrists is an ancient Chinese medicine acupressure point called the **Nei-Kuan point, also known as the Inner Gate point.** The band is designed to fit snugly around the wrist so that a button or disc in the band presses on this point. This pressure is said to affect the nerve pathway to the area of the brain that deals with motion sickness. Containing no medications, the wrist bands can be safely worn by children as well as by those who already are on medications for other conditions.

And then there are **natural products** for seasickness such as ginger root and peppermint. And, of course, a time-tested remedy when you feel sea sickness coming on is just to go up on deck to get some fresh air and to look out at the horizon.

I hope that the incidents you have where you experience a **topsy-turvy stomach and a strange and giddy head** will be few so that each cruise you take will be as enjoyable as possible.

Nautical Term

Bell Bottoms

Although there is some uncertainty about their origin, **it is believed that the first bell bottom pants were worn by men in the US Navy** – not by hippies in the 1960s. Mention is made in 1813 about blue trousers with bottoms shaped like bells being worn by sailors on US ships. **Bell bottom pants were a handy and functional design** -- easy to take off over boots, easy to roll up to avoid them becoming wet, and easy to remove and turn into a flotation device if the sailor fell into the sea.

Are Weddings Performed by Ship Captains Legal?

The gift shop of a ship we were on had a variety of humorous plaques for sale. One of them said, **"Passenger Alert! Any weddings performed by the captain of this ship are valid for the duration of the voyage only!"**

So what about ships and captains and weddings? Are weddings performed by ship captains legal? In an informal and very unscientific survey I conducted, I found that about half of the people I talked to thought that ship captains had the legal power to perform weddings. Another one-fourth thought that they did not, and the rest weren't sure.

Their answers to this question were probably influenced by their having read or seen ship captains in novels, movies, and TV shows perform weddings. For instance, do you remember the unusual wedding in the *Pirates of the Caribbean: At World's End* (the third movie in the series) where **Will** (Orlando Bloom) proposes and **Elizabeth** (Keira Knightley) accepts his proposal during an intense sword fight on board the ship? Without skipping a beat, the ship's captain, **Captain Hector Barbossa**

(Geoffrey Rush), who is also involved in the fight, quickly pronounces them man and wife right in the heat of the battle. This scene was great cinema, but was the wedding legal? Perhaps back then, some 400 years ago, it was. But would it be today? No, it would not.

In today's world, although the captain is the supreme authority on a ship, the mere fact that he or she is a ship's captain does not automatically give him or her legal certification to perform weddings. Modern laws in most parts of the world no longer endow a ship's captain with the power to perform a wedding.

Virtually all countries and jurisdictions now have specific laws and regulations about marriages. Whether a marriage is valid and whether the officiant (the one who performs the wedding) is legally authorized to do so **is a matter of domestic law from place to place and is subject to the requirements from country to country and, in the case of the United States, from state to state.**

Most cruise lines provide wedding packages as part of their cruises, packages that have been carefully developed and structured to allow passengers to have legal weddings while on a cruise. How and where these weddings take place can vary greatly from cruise line to cruise line and from ship to ship.

Some wedding packages provide for the wedding to take place **on the ship while at sea**, others **on the ship while docked at a port**, and others **at scenic and romantic places** like beaches, glaciers, and mountain tops. And, concerning the officiant, some packages say that **the captain will be the officiant** (and that the cruise line has taken steps so that the captain has the legal authority to do so), some specifically say that **the captain will not be the officiant**, and others indicate that **a local justice of the peace, minister, or notary public will perform the marriage**. In some cases, those being married are even allowed to bring along their own officiant.

And, of course, another important part of a legal wedding union is that the two people being married must meet the laws and rules required of them in the place they will be married – and that usually includes obtaining a wedding license from that jurisdiction. The wedding departments of the cruise lines are specialists in assisting with this – in helping the couple get the marriage license and in doing the other things needed for the wedding to take place in accordance with local laws. But all of this takes careful planning and advance preparation, so it is necessary to start the process well before the date of the cruise and to work closely with the wedding department of your cruise line on all the arrangements. Another suggestion is to make sure to **obtain your own legal advice in advance** to make sure that the wedding you are planning will, in fact, be recognized in your home jurisdiction.

So, can cruise ship captains perform legal weddings? Yes, they can -- but only some captains on some ships for some people in some locations.

Nautical Term

Scuttlebutt

When we talk about **scuttlebutt**, we mean gossipy information. This is another one of the many terms in use today that have a nautical origin. On old sailing ships, **the cask of drinking water was called a scuttled butt (and later a scuttlebutt)** and since sailors exchanged gossip and rumors when they gathered at the scuttlebutt for a drink of water, scuttlebutt became slang for gossip or rumors. A butt was a wooden cask which held water. To scuttle is to drill a hole to tap the cask.

Bow Thrusters – How Do You Parallel Park a Cruise Ship?

A friend of ours, when looking for a parking space, will sometimes drive a bit out of his way so he can find a spot that won't require him to parallel park his car between two other vehicles. A cruise ship captain, however, doesn't have that luxury available to him or her. The ship's parking spot (the berth) is pre-assigned by the port facility and there is no leeway in selecting another berth if other ships are already docked in front of or in back of that birth. **So the captains of cruise ships quite often have to parallel park their ship into relatively tight spots, often in the middle of a very busy harbor.** Docking a large ship is a difficult and often time-consuming process in any case, requiring a skilled captain, an experienced crew – and even tugboats in many instances.

Today, the process is simpler and faster than it used to be thanks to the wonderful invention of bow thrusters. **Essentially, bow thrusters are recessed propellers mounted sideways in the ship below the water level.** They are typically somewhat smaller than the ship's regular propellers and are used at slow speeds to help the ship maneuver in harbors and near docks. Although most of them are mounted in the bow (front) of the ship, thrusters can also be in other locations such as the stern. Technically, they are called **transversal propulsion devices** and can also be referred to as tunnel or transverse thrusters.

Bow Thrusters

A modern cruise ship, with its propellers and bow thrusters, can move forwards, backwards, and side to side. In order to dock the ship in a tight spot, the captain lines up the ship parallel with the space allotted to him and then **moves the ship sideways** until the ship is snug with the pier. This can be done in confined spaces as well as when there are significant winds and currents, thus making the docking process less time consuming, safer, and often eliminating the need for tugs.

Not all cruise ships have bow thrusters, but many of the newer ones do. As a passenger you may be able to tell if your ship has them as your ship docks and departs. Just look over the side and watch to see if there is a lot of swirling water at the side of the ship – and watch to see if your ship moves sideways. A large ship like the *Oasis of the Seas* has four bow thrusters, the *Sapphire Princess* has three bow thrusters and three stern thrusters, and the *Freedom of the Seas* has four bow thrusters on each side for a total of eight thrusters. Other types of ships also often have them, especially emergency vessels such as fire boats. Bow thrusters allow them to quickly move next to and to hold snug against a larger ship, such as a ferry boat, in order to evacuate passengers and take care of emergencies. Even pleasure boats may have small bow thrusters that help them maneuver and dock.

Sometimes thrusters are placed in tunnels that go sideways all the way through the ship. In these instances, as the bow thruster propeller moves, it takes suction and water from one side and throws it out the other side of the ship, thus moving the ship sideways. **This type of thruster can be operated in both directions and the propeller blades typically have a controllable pitch** (that is, the angle of the blades can be varied). As more or less thrust is needed, the pitch of the blades is changed rather than having to change the speed at which the propeller rotates.

All this is controlled from the bridge by the captain and his crew. **And many ships have bridges that extend out well beyond the side of the vessel to make it easy for those involved in docking to see exactly where the ship is in relation to the pier.** In fact, the floor of the bridge extension is often made of see-through glass so the captain can look directly downward.

Oh, and did you notice the bow thrusters in the movie *Poseidon* (the 2006 remake)? They played a role in helping some of those that were trapped to escape from inside the overturned ship.

Nautical Term

As the Crow Flies

Crows are fairly large, highly visible, and noisy birds that are **known to fly quite directly to a source of food** – as opposed to birds such as swallows that circle around a lot. So before the age of radar, ships often carried a cage of crows. When it was cloudy or a bit foggy and they weren't sure which way land was, **they would release a crow and watch which direction it flew, knowing that it would fly straight to land.** The lookout perch high on a sailing vessel became known as the **crow's nest** and the shortest distance between two points was **"as the crow flies."**

I Spy... a Lighthouse

As we traveled with our children when they were growing up, we enjoyed playing the game **"I Spy."** I remember how excited our youngest daughter was one time when it was her turn and she said, **"I spy with my little eye something that starts with the letter "L."** She had just spotted one of her favorite things off in the distance, **a lighthouse**, and was so eager to see if someone else could guess it. She has always had a special love for lighthouses, and even now, as a married adult with her own children, she still enjoys taking pictures of them and collecting lighthouse souvenirs.

For centuries, lighthouses have helped ships avoid danger. **However, because of the modern navigational systems onboard most of today's ships, lighthouses no longer play as critical a role as they once did in keeping ships safe.** But seeing them is still an enjoyable part of ship travel and I am always interested in knowing more about the ones I see.

According to the web site **"The Lighthouse Directory,"** there are more than **16,000 lighthouses worldwide.** While a large number of them are still operational, over the years many of them have been retired from active service and have become rundown and even unsafe. Some of these non-operational ones, if money has been available, have been refurbished and are now used as museums, gift shops, or for other purposes.

Cape Canaveral Lighthouse

So that ships can identify one lighthouse from another, both during the day and at night, **each lighthouse has unique characteristics.** (We'll use the Cape Canaveral lighthouse in Florida to help illustrate this.)

- **A Unique Physical Appearance - The various sizes, shapes, colors, and paint patterns of lighthouses set them apart,** which allows them to be recognized and identified during daylight hours. The Cape Canaveral lighthouse, for instance, is 151 feet tall, is shaped somewhat like a rocket, and has six broad alternating black and white horizontal bands painted on it. Even from a long distance, it is easy to identify this lighthouse.

- **A Distinctive Light Pattern at Night – Light patterns vary from lighthouse to lighthouse.** Many have lights that flash, while some are steady. Whereas most have white lights, there are some with colored lights. The Cape Canaveral lighthouse light pattern is two white flashes (separated by five seconds) every 20 seconds. At night, this distinctive light pattern helps sailors know that it is the Cape Canaveral lighthouse they are seeing.
- **Audible Signals –** In addition to their lights, **some lighthouses have audible signals such as fog horns or whistles to warn ships.** Typically, these devices are activated when the visibility in the area drops below a limit set for that location, such as several miles. The Cape Canaveral lighthouse, which sits a little bit inland, does not have any audible signals.

Reading about lighthouses can be fascinating, with many of them having interesting stories associated with them. A few that I particularly enjoyed reading about were:

- **The Lighthouse of Alexandria, Egypt** –Although it no longer exists, **this was one of the seven wonders of the ancient world.** At an estimated height of more than 390 feet, it was one of the tallest man-made structures on earth for a number of centuries.
- **The Rock of Gibraltar Lighthouse** – Called the Europa Point Light, this lighthouse is located on the Rock of Gibraltar at the southern tip of Spain where the Atlantic Ocean and the Mediterranean Sea meet. Prior to its opening in 1841, **sailors were dependent on the lights from the tower of a small Catholic church built on the rock** to navigate around this dangerous point of land.
- **Cape Horn Lighthouses** – These two important lighthouses at the tip of South America are **the southernmost lighthouses in the world.** They help

ships navigate some of the most dangerous shipping areas found anywhere.
- **The Sumiyoshi Lighthouse in Osaka, Japan** – Japan's oldest lighthouse, it was originally made out of wood. The current version is made of wood and stones. **The original lighthouse's light was fueled by rapeseed flower oil.** (The rapeseed flower is a member of the mustard or cabbage family and is the world's third largest source of vegetable oil.)
- **The Cape Canaveral Lighthouse in Florida** – **Werner von Braun**, the famous rocket scientist, used to stand on this lighthouse's platform to observe rocket launches at nearby Cape Canaveral. This is the only lighthouse that is owned by the United States Air Force. And, interestingly, if you want to telephone someone at the lighthouse, **the specially-assigned area code for Cape Canaveral is related to the space program. The area code is 3-2-1.**

Well, we could write so much more about lighthouses. I find them to be an interesting and charming part of sailing and love to see them wherever we travel.

Nautical Term

Know the Ropes

Old sailing ships had **complex systems of sails that were controlled by many ropes.** Sailors needed to **know the ropes** in order to hoist and lower the sails properly. Today, to **know the ropes** is to understand how to do something.

A Sanitation Score of 96... What Does That Mean?

As my wife and I were booking a recent cruise, we checked out the sanitation score of the ship we would be going on. We were pleased to find out that it received a score of 96 on its latest inspection. **So what does a score of 96 mean and who is it that does the sanitation inspections of cruise ships?**

Every cruise ship that has a foreign itinerary, visits US ports, and carries 13 or more passengers is subject to an unannounced twice-yearly inspection by the United States Centers for Disease Control and Prevention through their **Vessel Sanitation Program (VSP).** The primary purpose of the inspection is **to minimize the risk of gastrointestinal illnesses aboard vessels.**

Ships are rated on the sanitation of the following items:

- **Potable water systems**
- **Medical facilities**

- Swimming pools and whirlpool spas
- Galleys (kitchens) and dining rooms
- Child activity centers
- Hotel (stateroom) accommodations
- Ventilation systems
- Common areas of the ship

The ship is awarded points based on a 100-point rating system. Vessels that earn an 86 or higher score have a satisfactory sanitation level. Our ship, with a score of 96, was one of the highest-rated ones.

I recently went on-line to look at the latest VSP inspections, which are public information, and found a report covering 158 cruise ships. The ships achieved the following scores:

- **Score of 96 to 100 – 102 ships (32 had perfect scores of 100)**
- **Score of 91 to 95 – 38 ships**
- **Score of 86 to 90 – 13 ships**
- **Score of 85 or below – 5 ships (the lowest score was 69)**

The on-line information is quite detailed and indicates what caused the deductions, if any. For instance, on our ship there were two areas of concern:

- **Recreational Water Facilities** – Two points were deducted from our ship's possible score because "free residual halogen (bromine) was not recorded at the start or stop of shock halogenation for the whirlpools."
- **Dishwashing Equipment** – Two points were deducted because "the port-side dishwasher final rinse temperature gauge was not reading correctly. The gauge was reading 230°F and the inspector's thermometer measured 173°F."

By using your web browser to search for **Vessel Sanitation Program** you'll be able to see your cruise ship's score and learn more about this program, including how the inspections are conducted, how much the ships are charged for the inspections, and what the ships are required to do if a problem is discovered. I found it to be very interesting reading.

Nautical Term

Lido

Lido is a fashionable resort town near Venice in Northern Italy. **An Italian term meaning beach,** Lido is often used as the name for the deck on cruise ships where the outdoor swimming pools and surrounding recreational facilities are located.

Eggs Benedict at the Panama Canal

The 5th of February several years ago. 7:30 a.m. 84° Fahrenheit. Calm sea. A few puffy clouds. Pleasant breeze. Snowing back home. Aboard a modern cruise ship. Stateroom with a verandah. Up early relaxing in our lounge chairs on our own private balcony. Complimentary bathrobes and slippers. Room service. **Eggs Benedict and freshly squeezed orange juice.** Linen napkins. The first set of locks of the Panama Canal sliding past us. Our ship just a few feet from the side of one of the locks. **Not a care in the world!**

Comfortable room. Pleasant night's sleep. All the food one could want -- all the time. Enjoyable entertainment every night of the cruise. Interesting fellow passengers. Beautiful scenery. Colorful ports of call. A special low-cost deal from our travel agent.

Now this is cruising!

Our cruise ship is a Panamax – a ship built specially to conform to the maximum dimensions possible for passage through the Panama Canal. Any ship longer than 294 meters

(964.56 feet) and wider than 32.2 meters (105.97 feet) won't fit in the locks. Our journey from the Atlantic to the Pacific side of Panama will take eight or nine hours and will cover just 51 miles. **But using the canal shaves off over 7,800 miles between New York City and San Francisco.**

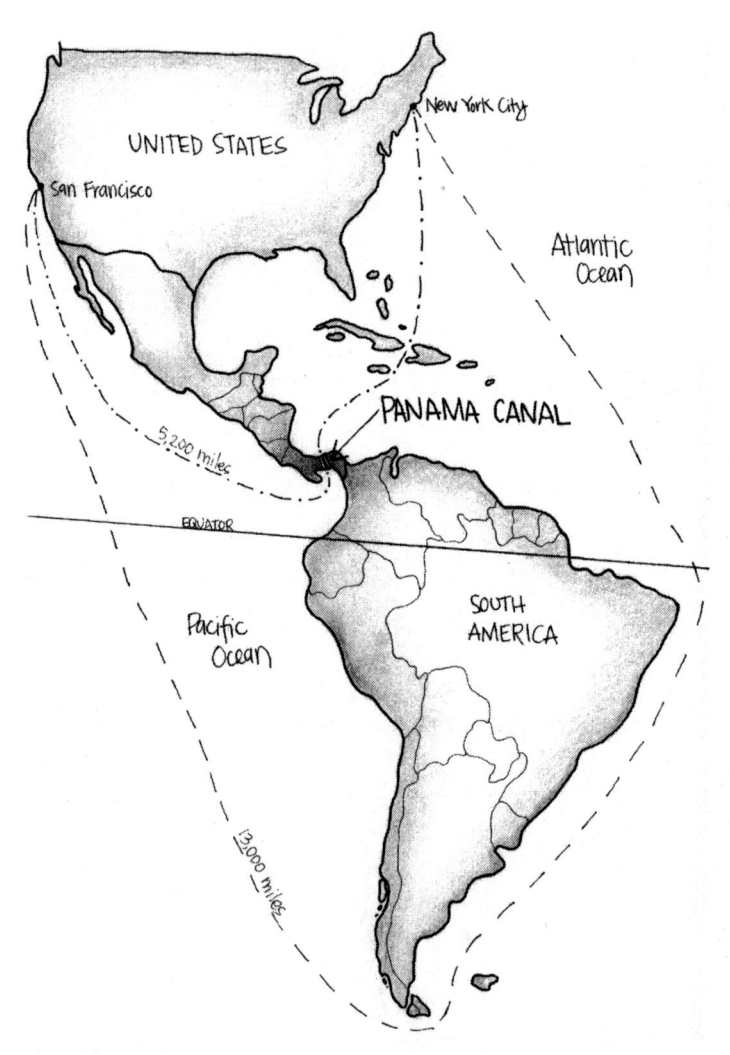

The Panama Canal opened in 1914. Since then thousands of ships have passed through its locks each year. And what does it cost to go through the canal? The toll for using the canal varies with the vessel type, size, and cargo -- **with one of the highest tolls ever paid being more than $375,000 for one passage.**

In order to improve the canal and keep up with changes in the worldwide shipping industry, **a major Panama Canal expansion project is presently underway.** At a cost of over $6 billion and climbing, much larger additional locks are being built and the canal is being widened. Completion is scheduled for 2015 or 2016. The new canal will enable many of the latest mega ships -- large resort ships, cargo ships, and oilers to pass through it, more than doubling the capacity of the canal. The new locks are a modern engineering marvel utilizing new designs, materials, and techniques to move the ships more rapidly and efficiently through the canal. Tugboats instead of locomotives will now position the vessels in the locks and the new lock system will use gravity and valves to raise and lower the water rather than using pumps.

There are hundreds of cruise ship itineraries available today, but one that I would definitely recommend to you is the Panama Canal. And if you decide to go on a Panama Canal cruise, you may want to splurge by booking a stateroom with an outdoor verandah – **so you can be eating Eggs Benedict on your own private balcony while passing through the Panama Canal.**

Nautical Term

Manifest

An important document on ships, airplanes, and other vehicles is the manifest, especially the passenger manifest. When used as a verb, manifest means to make things evident, to clearly show things, and to openly list things. As a noun it is a detailed listing of all passengers, crew, and cargo so that customs and other government officials have a clear understanding of who and what is being transported. **The manifest is required by law.** In the case of a cruise ship, this document is created at the start of a voyage and is presented to ports along the way. The captain of the ship is responsible for maintaining its accuracy and he or she is accountable at the end of the voyage **to make sure that everyone and everything on the manifest is properly accounted for.**

What Is Pod Propulsion?

Pod propulsion is a fascinating and relatively new way to propel a ship. Let's use an actual example – the Queen Mary 2 (QM2), which began service in January 2004 – to illustrate what we are talking about.

Instead of having propellers attached to propeller shafts that poke out from the underside of the ship, the QM2 has **four large pods** suspended beneath the aft (rear) area of the hull. As can be seen in the illustration, **the pods look somewhat like miniature submarines**. Two of the pods, the ones more forward on the hull, are fixed in place. The two other pods at the rear are **azimuthing**, meaning that they can rotate in either direction a full 360 degrees – at least that's their rotation capability in the case of the QM2. A single large stainless steel propeller, nearly 20 feet in diameter, is attached to each pod.

Interestingly enough **the propellers face forward**, not to the rear of the ship. The propellers **pull the ship through the water** rather than pushing it. The advantage of pulling is that the revolving blades bite into what is described as clean water rather than disturbed water. Disturbed water that passes through a propeller circumference weakens performance and encourages vibration.

The pod's "engine room" is not even inside the ship. The huge electric motor that drives each propeller is **inside the pod.** The two azimuthing pods furthest to the rear of the vessel steer and maneuver the ship -- **so no rudder is needed on the Queen Mary 2.** And the necks of the pods are large enough to accommodate a ladder that extends from inside the ship down into each pod so that a worker can climb down to inspect and maintain the equipment – but only while the ship is moored.

So how well does pod propulsion work? **If engineered and outfitted properly, it significantly cuts down on noise and vibrations – and it is a more efficient propulsion system.** And in the case of the QM2, it propels that large, beautiful ocean liner at a very rapid top speed of approximately **30 miles per hour.**

There actually are three additional propeller-type devices on the QM2, for a total of seven. These three additional ones, facing sideways and located near the front of the ship, are called **bow thrusters**. Bow thrusters are discussed in Article 5.

Pod Propulsion

Nautical Term

Muster

One of the things that cruise passengers do soon after first boarding their ship is to assemble near the life boats and **muster** at their **muster stations.** From the Latin word, **monstrate, meaning to show,** the nautical usage of this term goes back to the early days of seafaring when the entire ship's company was commanded **to muster, or show, on deck** for a roll call of names. Among other things, this helped ensure that everyone on board was properly accounted for so that no one could use a fictitious name, or some other ploy, to get a double issue of rations or pay. Today mustering serves as a roll call and as a time to provide safety instructions to the new passengers.

Smokestacks on the Titanic

The story is told that when **J. Bruce Ismay**, the chairman and managing director of White Star Lines, inspected the scale model of the ship that his company was planning to build, he was confused. **He had been told that the ocean liner, to be named the RMS Titanic, was to have three engines, but the scale model showed that the ship would have four funnels or smokestacks.** He asked the ship's architect, "Why four funnels? Don't we only have three engines?" To this the architect replied, "The Mauretania and the Lusitania both have four funnels and we didn't think that you would want your ship to have less. **The extra funnel will make the ship look more powerful and majestic and it will give people the impression that the ship can go faster."**

So the Titanic, **the largest movable object built by mankind up to that time,** was built with four smokestacks – one of them being a dummy. The extra one's only function was to provide ventilation for the engine rooms and kitchen galleys. The Titanic was massive. It had 29 boilers, 159 furnaces, and three gigantic propellers. When cruising at sea, it used **850 tons of coal per day.**

The primary purpose of funnels on older ships was to allow smoke, heat, and excess steam to escape from the boiler rooms. As time went by and ship engines and fuels changed and improved, the size, shape, and number of funnels on ships became more symbolic of speed, power, and style than they were an engineering necessity. Usually painted in the house colors of the shipping company **(the Titanic's were bronze with a black band at the top)**, the funnels became part of the distinctive look and image that the company wanted to portray.

Today, funnels still play an important role, but normally just one funnel on a ship is sufficient and it doesn't need to be nearly as large as those in the past – **and it doesn't particularly need to look like a smokestack.** Just picture in your mind the various modern cruise ships you have seen on your ocean journeys and it will be evident that ship architects have become very creative when it comes to designing funnels that hardly look like smokestacks.

And here are a few random bits of information about funnels:
- **The smokestacks on the Titanic were large enough to drive two locomotives through at the same time.** They were so big **(they weighed 60 tons each)** that they had cables running down to the deck to help hold them in place in case of rough seas.
- **The SS Great Eastern,** launched in 1858, was the only ship to have **five funnels.**
- **Ladders were built inside of the smokestacks on many older ships.** They provided emergency escape routes to the outside for the stokers and engineers in case the ship was foundering and the watertight doors below deck were closed.
- **On the Disney Magic and the Disney Fantasy, the forward funnel is a false one.** The AquaDuck water coaster goes right through the forward funnel and the ship's exclusive club for tweens (ages 11-14), called The Edge, is located inside the funnel.
- **The Oasis of the Seas has retractable telescoping funnels.** Retracting them was necessary so the ship

could pass under Denmark's Great Belt Fixed Link Bridge as the Oasis of the Seas traveled from the shipyard in Finland where it was built out into the open sea.

And a post script relating to the Titanic. **Titanic II, a full-size replica of the original ocean liner, is being talked about.** Reportedly, an Australian businessman is behind the possible project. The idea is to re-create the details of the original RMS Titanic as closely as possible on the new ship. **And, of course, it is planned to have four huge funnels.**

Nautical Term

Square Meal

Big square wooden platters were once used to serve the meals on many old vessels. Virtually unbreakable, the platters were easy to stack and stow in racks between meals and they were large enough to provide an ample amount of food for the hungry sailors. Today, a meal that is complete and substantial is referred to as a **square meal.**

Do You Remember Gopher, Your Yeoman Purser?

A major character on the Love Boat series that ran for nine years on television was Burl "Gopher" Smith, Your Yeoman Purser. Do you remember him? Played by **Fred Grandy**, (see the end of the article for some trivia about him) he was responsible for helping take care of the needs of the passengers so they could experience a pleasant cruise and vacation.

As the purser, Gopher was continually involved in unusual, difficult, comical, and quirky situations. He was known as "Your Yeoman Purser," a designation implying his diligence, dependability, and service-oriented attitude in carrying out his duties, often under difficult and amusing circumstances.

For instance, I remember one episode where bouquet after bouquet of flowers and handful after handful of cablegrams kept arriving at the ship for delivery to one of the female passengers. Try as he might, Gopher, the purser, just couldn't figure out how to fit them all into her cabin. In another episode, Gopher innocently caused trouble when he brought a pet chimpanzee onto the ship – a chimp that turned out to have a propensity for stealing things from the passengers and crew.

Pursers have been part of ships for many centuries. The word is derived from the word purse and signifies one who is in charge of the money. **In earlier years, they were in charge of paying the crew and for selling supplies to the crew such as food, drink, clothing, and bedding.** Today's cruise ship pursers, and their multi-person staffs, usually work from a desk or counter near the main atrium or lobby of the ship. The services they provide to passengers include the following:

- Answering questions
- Resolving problems
- Handling passenger accounts
- Exchanging foreign currency
- Dealing with complaints
- Dispensing seasick pills
- Acting as the post office
- Providing lost and found

Whether this group on your particular ship is known as **the purser's office, the customer service department, guest relations, or the hospitality desk,** the services they perform are of great benefit to you as a passenger and are essential to the success of the cruise line.

And here is some trivia about **Fred Grandy (Gopher):**

- He was the roommate of **David Eisenhower** (grandson of Pres. Dwight D. Eisenhower) at Phillips Exeter Academy and was best man at David's wedding to Julie Nixon (daughter of Pres. Richard M. Nixon)
- He graduated in English studies from **Harvard University**
- He speaks **English, French, and Arabic**
- He was elected to the **US House of Representatives from Iowa** in 1986 and served for four terms
- He was captain and CEO of **Goodwill Industries International** for five years

Nautical Term

Doldrums

Having been around ships a lot, I smiled the other day when the reporter on a sports radio station described a team as being in the doldrums ever since they lost the championship. **To be in the doldrums, of course, means to be in a dull, listless, and depressed mood.** The term doldrums stems from a section of the ocean where it was common for the winds to stop, sometimes for days at a time, thereby stranding sailing ships. **Officially, the doldrums is a portion of the Atlantic Ocean and the Pacific Ocean affected by the Intertropical Convergence Zone, a low-pressure area around the equator where the prevailing winds often are calm.**

Nautical Term

Doldrums

Having been around ships a lot, I smiled the other day when the reporter on a sports radio station described a team as being in the doldrums ever since they lost the championship. **To be in the doldrums, of course, means to be in a dull, listless, and depressed mood.** The term doldrums stems from a section of the ocean where it was common for the winds to stop, sometimes for days at a time, thereby stranding sailing ships. **Officially, the doldrums is a portion of the Atlantic Ocean and the Pacific Ocean affected by the Intertropical Convergence Zone, a low-pressure area around the equator where the prevailing winds often are calm.**

Whether this group on your particular ship is known as **the purser's office, the customer service department, guest relations, or the hospitality desk,** the services they perform are of great benefit to you as a passenger and are essential to the success of the cruise line.

And here is some trivia about **Fred Grandy (Gopher):**

- He was the roommate of **David Eisenhower** (grandson of Pres. Dwight D. Eisenhower) at Phillips Exeter Academy and was best man at David's wedding to Julie Nixon (daughter of Pres. Richard M. Nixon)
- He graduated in English studies from **Harvard University**
- He speaks **English, French, and Arabic**
- He was elected to the **US House of Representatives from Iowa** in 1986 and served for four terms
- He was captain and CEO of **Goodwill Industries International** for five years

The "Ests" of Cruise Ships

I am amazed at the size and magnificence of cruise ships. They keep getting bigger and better with an ever-increasing array of facilities and activities. Let's take a look at some of the "ests" of today's cruise ships – the new**est**, the larg**est**, the long**est**, the high**est**-rated, and the fast**est**. (Please note that the ships we've compared in these "ests" are only large cruise ships of at least 100,000 gross tons. The lists are current as of mid-2014.)

Newest Large Ships
1. **Regal Princess** (Princess Cruise Line) – Put into service in May 2014
2. **Norwegian Getaway** (Norwegian Cruise Line) – Put into service in January 2014
3. **Royal Princess** (Princess Cruise Line) – Put into service in June 2013

There are several additional large cruise ships currently under construction for delivery later in 2014 and in 2015.

Largest by Gross Tonnage
1. **(Tie) Allure of the Seas** (Royal Caribbean International) – 225,282 GT (6,360 passengers)
2. **(Tie) Oasis of the Seas** (Royal Caribbean International) – 225,282 GT (6,360 passengers) This is the sister ship to Allure of the Seas.
3. **Norwegian Epic** (Norwegian Cruise Line) – 155,873 GT (5,400 passengers)

In determining the size of a ship, the volume of a ship (its gross tonnage) is calculated rather than weighing it. Gross tonnage (GT) is a measurement of the **enclosed space** within a ship's hull and superstructure. The largest ship ever built, an oil tanker named the **Seawise Giant**, which is no longer in service, had a gross tonnage of 260,941.

Longest
1. **Allure of the Seas** (Royal Caribbean International) – 1,187+ feet (This ship is two inches longer than the Oasis of the Seas. It unintentionally ended up being built just a bit longer.)
2. **Oasis of the Seas** (Royal Caribbean International) – 1,187 feet
3. **Queen Mary 2** (Cunard Line) – 1,132 feet (Technically, the QM2 is a transatlantic ocean liner rather than a cruise ship.)

By comparison, the **Titanic** was 883 feet long and the **Mayflower** was estimated to be between 100 and 110 feet in length. Ships are measured from the very tip of their bow to the farthest point aft on their stern.

Highest-Rated Large Ships
1. **Queen Mary 2** (Cunard Line)
2. **Celebrity Reflection** (Celebrity Cruises)
3. **Celebrity Silhouette** (Celebrity Cruises)

Considering only cruise ships of 100,000 GT or more, the above three ships received **the highest scores from Berlitz, which is a highly-respected rater of cruise ships.** The Berlitz evaluation system takes five areas into account: accommodations, food, service, entertainment, and the overall cruise experience.

Fastest Large Ships
1. **Queen Mary 2** (Cunard Line) – 30 knots
2. **A number of ships are runners-up to the QM2,** which is clearly the fastest large cruise ship or ocean liner. The runner-up ships have cruising speeds in the 22-26 knot range with top speeds several knots above that.

And in answer to the frequently asked question of whether or not cruise ships are fast enough to pull water skiers, the answer is yes -- but only if the skier can keep holding on to the tow rope until the ship is going fast enough to get the skier up out of the water. Water skiing is typically done in the range of 12 to 30 knots, **so large ships at their cruising speeds would certainly be going fast enough.** And wouldn't their wakes make for some interesting water skiing and wake boarding?

Is Bigger Better?
So when it comes to cruise ships, is bigger better? People have their own opinion about that. Personally, I like the variety of ship sizes that are available. I love the new gigantic mega-ships and all that they offer. And I also love the personal feel and quieter ambience of the smaller ships. I guess I just love cruise ships. How about you?

Nautical Term

Figureheads

A wonderful design element of old sailing ships was **the figurehead attached to the prow of the vessel.** (The prow is the foremost part of the ship – the part of the bow above the waterline.) Usually a large and colorful wooden carving (often of a woman), the figurehead was a unique design for each ship that helped identify the vessel. It also was a status symbol, indicating the owner's wealth and power. Today, of course, a figurehead is someone at the head of a country or organization who is very visible but who doesn't have much actual power and authority.

One Crew Member's Employment Contract

Many cruise ship passengers are curious about the crew on the ship and how they get hired, what they get paid, where they live, and other details about their employment. Let's take a look at one cruise ship employee – **an orchestra musician on a large ship** – to see what kind of employment situation he has.

Jason (not his real name) played trumpet in his high school and college marching bands. He also was a member of several instrumental groups during those years. Besides the trumpet, he plays the guitar, saxophone, and keyboard. He knows many music types, can sight read, and is good at improvising. As Jason finished college, he wanted to earn money using his musical skills. He also wanted to travel. A friend suggested he contact an employment agency his friend knew of that specialized in placing musicians and entertainers on cruise ships, in casinos, and in luxury hotels.

Jason, who lives on the West Coast, filled out the employment agency's on-line application, sent in a resume and an audition tape, and was invited to Los Angeles to do a 30-minute in-person audition. **The agency liked him, was** impressed with his musical abilities, and four weeks later Jason was offered employment with a major cruise line as an orchestra musician on one of their ships. Jason signed their multi-page employment contract and six weeks later found himself working on a beautiful cruise ship that sails the Caribbean out of a port in Florida. Here are some of the details of Jason's employment:

- **Job Title and Description** – Jason is an **orchestra musician** (also called a show band musician or a sideman). Orchestra musicians perform at and support all main stage performances on the ship, such as the big production shows. They also back up guest entertainers and provide the music for cabaret acts, dance events, cocktail parties with the captain, and talent shows.

- **Lodging** – Jason shares a **small crew cabin** on a lower deck of the ship with one other orchestra musician. The cabin has two bunk beds, a desk, chair, television, wardrobe, and bathroom. It is similar to the passenger cabins on the rest of the ship except that the furnishings are simpler and the cabin is smaller.

- **Pay** – The starting pay (in 2014) for an orchestra musician on the ship is from **$1,800 to $2,200 per month**. Jason, because of his varied musical talents, is started at $1,925. Pay day is once per month and he is paid in US cash. (Most of the crew prefers receiving cash.) His lodging, food, and access to a free laundry are provided as part of his contract.

- **Contract Length** – He signed a **six-month contract**. The cruise line hopes that he will extend his employment beyond that time and they have told Jason that if he does so he will receive an increase in pay. The contract talks specifically about what were to happen if Jason quits before the six months are up or if his performance as an orchestra musician is unsatisfactory. If either of these were to happen, he would have to pay his own way home and would not be rehired by the ship.

- **Hours** – Jason is expected to work **seven days a week**, if necessary, for as many hours as he is needed. He does not punch a time clock and there is no overtime pay.

- **Food and Leisure** – Jason normally eats his meals **in the crew cafeteria** and spends a lot of his off-duty time in the facilities set aside just for the crew – a lounge, game room, bar, small swimming pool, and gym. Although his food is covered by his employment, his drinks are not.

- **Where He May Go on the Ship** – **As an entertainer, Jason has more latitude and freedom on the ship than many other crew members have,** but he is specifically restricted by his employment contract from going into passenger cabins, the casino, and the passenger swimming pools. He may eat at the passenger buffet at certain times and have a drink at a table in a passenger lounge, but, interestingly, **he is not allowed to sit on bar stools**. Also, he may not walk around the ship with a drink and/or a cigarette in his hand. He has a

curfew – 1:00 a.m. in the public passenger areas and 3:00 a.m. in the crew areas.
- **May He Go Ashore When the Ship is in Port?** – Yes, he and other members of the crew are allowed to go ashore when the ship visits a port, unless they have responsibilities on board.
- **What about Leave?** Jason is given **unpaid leave** between his contracts, with the ship paying for his transportation home and back to the ship.

So far, Jason enjoys what he does and fits in well as an orchestra musician. He thinks he would like to work several years with the cruise line before settling down back home. When asked what his biggest challenge is in being an orchestra musician, he laughs and says, **"Trying to hit the right notes on the trumpet when I am seasick."**

Nautical Term

Mind Your Ps and Qs

There are several theories about how this phrase originated. One of them has to do with sailors. **A tally of pints and quarts (Ps and Qs) consumed by each sailor at waterfront pubs and taverns was typically kept by the bartender on a chalkboard near the bar.** Before going ashore, the sailors were admonished by the captain to **"mind their Ps and Qs"** as they were drinking to make sure that the bartender didn't sneak a few extra marks on the board, thus inflating the bill.

Stretching the Ship – and the Revenue

Let's see now, how could we increase the revenue we receive from our cruise ship by a large amount, say by about 15%? Maybe we could raise the cruise rates to all of our customers, but that would probably price us out of the market. **Well, then, how about stretching our ship and adding 151 more staterooms?** Yeah, let's do that.

That is exactly what Royal Caribbean did to the **Enchantment of the Seas** in 2005, and what other cruise lines have done to some of their ships. In the case of Enchantment of the Seas, the number of staterooms was increased **from 975 to 1,126** and the length of the ship went from **917 feet to 990 feet.** The additional cabins gave revenues a big boost and the added area allowed the swimming pool to be increased in size by 50% and the ship to have even more recreational amenities and public space.

So how does one stretch a ship? By cutting it in half and adding a larger mid-section. **And how long does it take?** Around four to six weeks assuming the new mid-section has already been built and is waiting to be installed. **And what does**

it cost? In the case of Enchantment of the Seas, the cost was about $60 million, which is just a fraction of what it would cost to build a new cruise ship.

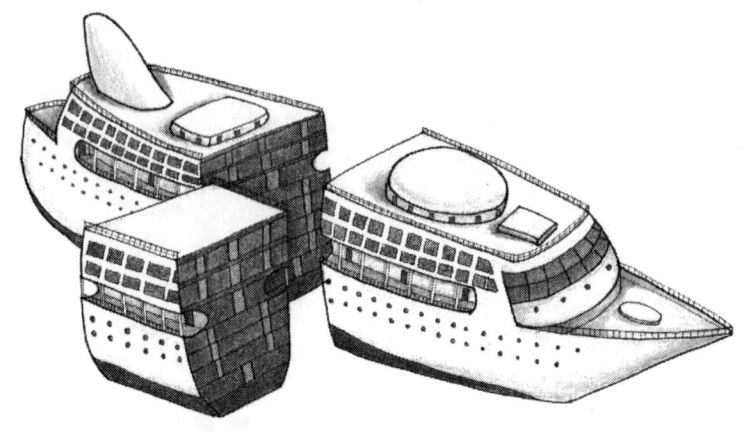

The stretching of the ship is accomplished by putting the ship in dry dock and literally cutting the ship down the middle – all the way from the top deck to the bottom of the hull. One of the halves is moved away from the other one and then the new mid-section is slid into place. The two halves are nudged up to the new section and then everything is carefully welded together. The service-type things are plugged in and connected. Cables, electrical lines, pipes, air ducts, and sewer lines are attached and tested, and finally carpeting, wall sections, ceiling sections, and such, are put in place to cover up where the ship's sections come together. **When you're all done with that, you let water back into the dry dock, test out the ship in open water, and put it back into service.** For Enchantment of the Seas, it was back in operation **within six weeks of going into dry dock.**

And what about the performance of the ship? Is it affected by all of this? Yes, but usually not in major ways. By way of computer simulation, engineers can determine quite accurately in advance what they need to do to keep the ship operating properly and smoothly after it has been stretched. Enchantment of the Seas needed some rudder modifications and some increased bow thruster output, and then it was good to go.

In fact, in some ways the new ship is said to perform even better than the old one. In the cruise industry, **bigger is better,** as evidenced by the many huge new ships that have come into the market recently. Of course, for many travelers **smaller is best,** so there will always be plenty of small and medium-sized ships around to satisfy those who prefer a more intimate and private experience.

Nautical Term

Feeling Blue

If you are unhappy or discouraged and you say that you are **feeling blue,** many etymologists believe you are using an old maritime phrase that dates back to the days of ocean-going sailing vessels. If the death of the captain or an officer occurred during the voyage, **the ship would hoist blue flags and paint a blue stripe along the length of the entire hull** when returning to its home port as a sign to other ships and to the people in port that a tragedy had taken place.

How Are You at "Sending the Biscuit?"

My wife is really good at **"sending the biscuit."** Her skill with **the tang and the biscuit** allows her to win nearly every shuffleboard game we play when we are on cruises. How about you? **How are your shuffleboard skills?**

Shuffleboard is an old game that originated indoors with coins and long tables. Even the famous **King Henry VIII** played shuffleboard (called **shovelboard,** or sometimes **shovillaborde,** back then). He played it with large coins on his long wooden dining table after dinner. We know this because it is recorded in the royal ledger kept during his reign that **he wagered and lost £9 (9 English pounds)** to a certain Lord William during a shovelboard game in 1532.

Shuffleboard made the jump from dining tables, taverns, and other venues to ocean liner decks in the 1840s. Back then the **Peninsular and Oriental Line (the P&O Line)** asked its recreation directors to think of games that passengers could enjoy while on their ships and one of them got the idea to transform shuffleboard so it could be played on the decks of their ocean liners. Disks **(called biscuits)** replaced the coins and long sticks **(called tangs)** were used to propel the weights along the wooden decks. Markings painted on the court determined the scoring.

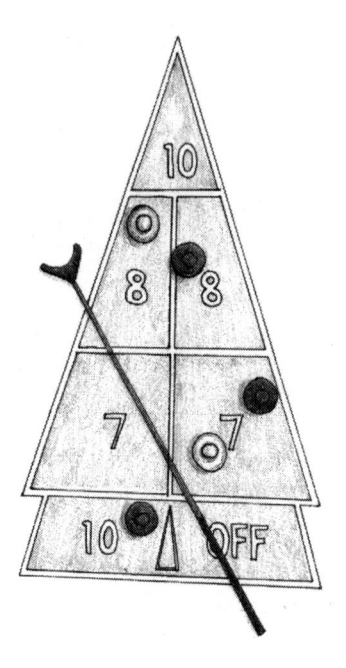

As the game's popularity grew, it became a must-have on ocean liners. When I was just five years old, our family went from New York City to Rotterdam on Holland America's ship, the Nieuw Amsterdam. Then four years later, we returned from England to New York on Cunard's Queen Mary. I loved the time we spent on those ships and, along with the amazing food, one of my lasting memories from those trips was playing shuffleboard up on deck with my parents and siblings. Today, I am happy that shuffleboard is still available on most cruise ships because I find it very enjoyable and relaxing – and because it is a great tradition. **I am a bit old fashioned when it comes to sailing, and it is my personal feeling that a cruise ship can't really be considered to be one of the great ones unless biscuits, tangs, and shuffleboard are part of the experience.**

Let's review the **terminology and rules** of the game:
- **Biscuits** – Each player has **four biscuits** (or pucks, or weights, or disks). The player with the lighter-colored ones (usually yellow or red) goes first. The other disks normally are black.
- **Tang** – The pole used to push the biscuits is called a **tang** (or stick, or cue) and is made out of metal or wood. It has a half-circle attachment or opening on one end of it to fit the biscuits.
- **Court** – A regulation shuffleboard court is 36 feet long and six feet wide. The large triangular areas at each end contain the numbers **10, 8, 8, 7, 7, and 10 off.**
- **Frames** – The players take turns sending one biscuit at a time down the court. **A frame is when all eight biscuits have been played.** Play ends when one player reaches 75 points or when both players have completed 10 frames, whichever comes first.
- **Scoring** – To score, a biscuit must end up entirely within the scoring area at the conclusion of the frame. **If any part of the biscuit is touching a line, it does not count.** (When my wife and I play, we change this rule. We say that if more than half of a biscuit is in the numbered area, we count it. Otherwise, we would hardly ever score.)
- **Strategy** – It is okay to knock the opponent's biscuits out of the scoring zone by hitting them with your own biscuit. **Doing so is not being mean to your opponent.** Doing so is good strategy and is an expected part of the game. (These last comments are specifically directed to my wife who thinks it is rude when I knock her biscuits out of the scoring area. But when she does it to me, she thinks it is fine.)

My wife has already challenged me to another shuffleboard match on our next cruise. I'd better practice up, because, as I said at the beginning, she's really good at **"sending the biscuit."**

Nautical Term

Barge In

It is considered poor manners **to barge in** -- that is to interrupt, break into, or interfere with someone else's activity. This phrase comes from the world of ships and shipping. **A barge is a bulky, low-slung freight boat, normally flat-bottomed, which is difficult to steer, maneuver, and control.** It is not uncommon for barges to bump into or interfere with other boats **(to barge in)** as the barge is moving along a waterway or is docking.

Are Ships Still Christened?

Are ships still christened? **Yes they are -- and with just as much pomp, ceremony, and fanfare as in the old days.**

The christening of ships is a tradition going back thousands of years. Resembling early religious customs and later the Christian rite of baptism, **christening often involved the breaking of a bottle of liquid, normally champagne or wine, over the bow of the ship.** The christening ceremony was meant to bring good fortune to the vessel and to those who operated it and sailed on it.

In the past several hundred years, it has become tradition in Great Britain and the US to often have females christen ships. **Royalty, media stars, politicians, or significant people in the news have been given this honor** and in many cases the females who did so were named as the godmother of the ship.

Among the thousands of ship christenings and launchings that have taken place over the years, here are a few of my personal favorites:

- **British Princesses** - If you are the Princess Cruise Line, you'd of course look for an opportunity to have real princesses christen some of your ships. In November

1984 in Southampton, England, **Princess Diana, the Princess of Wales,** christened the line's new cruise ship named the **Royal Princess.** Then in June 2013, the ship they built to replace the one introduced in 1984 was christened by **Princess Kate, the Duchess of Cambridge.** This new ship is also called the **Royal Princess.**

- **Super-sized Bottle of Champagne** – In 1995, **the largest bottle of champagne ever made up to that point in time** was used to christen **the Legend of the Seas** of the Royal Caribbean International Line. Equivalent to the size of 34 normal bottles, this special bottle of Moët & Chandon champagne was quite a hit (pun intended) on that occasion.

- **Pixy Dust** – In 1999, **Tinkerbell** became the first animated character to christen a ship. She broke a bottle of champagne against the hull of **the Disney Wonder** and then finished up the ceremony by **sprinkling pixy dust on the ship.**
- **Mercury Astronaut's Wife** – When Celebrity Cruises launched their new ship, **the Mercury**, they appropriately invited **Astronaut Scott Carpenter's wife, Patricia Barrett Carpenter,** to christen the ship. (Scott Carpenter, who was one of the original seven **Mercury** astronauts, was the second US astronaut to orbit the earth.)
- **Prohibition Era** – During the prohibition era (1920 to 1933), a number of ships in the US were christened with **water, cider, and other non-alcoholic beverages.**
- **The Non-Christening** – And who christened the **Titanic?** No one. It was never christened. It was not the practice of the ship's owners, **the White Star Line**, to hold such ceremonies for any of their ships.

Christening is an important event in the completion of a ship and today it still is a **festive, exciting, and well-publicized occasion,** often with bunting, decorations, bands, speeches, fireworks, and food being part of the big celebration.

Nautical Term

Navy Blue

As you know, **navy blue** is a very dark shade of the color blue which appears as almost black. **It got its name from the uniforms worn by British naval officers beginning in the mid-1700s which were dark blue and white.** First known as marine blue, the color later became known as navy blue.

Today it is often shortened to just one word – **navy** – rather than navy blue.

What Is the Status of Fire Safety on Cruise Ships?

Some months ago, an unfortunate thing happened on a large cruise ship in the Gulf of Mexico. A fire broke out in the aft engine room of the ship as it was on the third day of a four-day cruise of the Western Caribbean. The fire was extinguished and no crew members or passengers were injured. Because of the fire, the ship lost its propulsion and electricity (except for emergency electricity) and ended up adrift 150 miles off the Yucatan Peninsula. Several tug boats were sent to the aid of the ship and they slowly towed it to Mobile, Alabama where the passengers were finally able to disembark several days after the incident.

The International Convention for the Safety of Life at Sea (SOLAS) is a maritime treaty that is the most important of all international agreements concerning the safety of ships. SOLAS came into being in 1914 shortly after the sinking of the Titanic in 1912. It has been regularly updated and amended since then. **Nearly all countries have agreed to abide by its requirements and all cruise ships fall under its regulations.**

In broad terms, SOLAS requires ships to comply with minimum safety standards in three areas: **construction, equipment, and operation.** Among the specific areas covered by SOLAS are the design and construction of ships, **fire safety on board,** life saving equipment and procedures, communications, rules of navigation, cargo handling, and security.

Fires on board ships are a major safety concern in the industry. The old sailing ships of several hundred years ago were beautiful to see, but they were horrible at fire safety. Almost all parts of those ships (the wood hull, wood decks, masts, sails, furnishings, etc.) were combustible. Many fire tragedies took place on those ships. In the mid-1800s when metal hulls, metal structural pieces, and metal decks began being used, the fire safety of ships was greatly enhanced.

Over the years, improved fire safety for ships has been an ongoing process. SOLAS regulations have been continually revised to respond to new technology and to what the shipping industry learns each time there is a problem on a ship. Today, the regulations are numerous and very detailed, **leading to a high level of safety and security on ships.**

Among the regulations relating to fire, a number of significant new ones came into being in 1997:

- Smoke detectors and smoke alarms have to be present in all passenger cabins, crew cabins, and in all public spaces.
- Emergency alarms have to be audible in all cabins.
- All stairways have to be enclosed in self-contained fire zones.
- All fire doors throughout the ship have to be controllable from the navigation bridge.
- Low-level lighting showing routes of escape have to be placed in corridors, stairways, and public places.

Additionally, SOLAS now requires the elimination of nearly all combustible materials on ships. (Non-combustible material is defined as material that will not ignite, burn, support combustion, or release flammable vapors when subject to fire or heat.) In particular, this means that the materials that go into the construction of ship cabins – wall panels, ceiling panels, furniture, floor coverings, draperies, etc. – have to be non-combustible. The same applies to all other areas of the ship including dining rooms, theatres, galleys, lounges, stairways, hallways, decks, engine rooms, etc. **October 1, 2010 was set as the deadline for ships to be in compliance with all SOLAS regulations,** which meant that many existing ships had to be remodeled and upgraded by that date to meet the requirements. That has been accomplished. Today's cruise ships all are in compliance with the combustible materials regulations of SOLAS.

As a passenger, you may have noticed **some of the effects of SOLAS fire regulations.** For instance:

- **Real wood** has been disappearing from cruise ship decks, railings, wall paneling, and furniture and has been replaced by other safer materials.

- The parading of **flaming desserts** such as Baked Alaska, Bananas Foster, and Cherries Jubilee through the dining room has disappeared for the most part -- although we have still seen some dessert parades, now with battery-operated blinking electric lights on the dessert platters.
- Because open flames are not allowed in the galley, **steaks and other meats** are now typically cooked using other cooking methods, such as induction cooking.

Even though these requirements may have taken away some of the wonderful old charm of cruising, I am appreciative to the industry for being so sensitive to fire safety. **Above all, I want my family and your family to be as safe as possible when they go on cruises.**

Nautical Term

Leeward

Leeward refers to the side of a ship (or to the side of an island) that is sheltered from the wind. The opposite of leeward is windward. Ships tend to list (lean) toward the leeward as they are sailing.

18

Turn Down That Rock-n-Roll!

A travel agent told me about a client of hers who hasn't been on a cruise for over 20 years. **The client tried one cruise, but vowed to never go on another one because of the rock and roll. And this client wasn't talking about the loud music of the 1950s, but about the movements of the ship that made her seasick.** The cruise ship that the lady went on all those years ago was a smaller one in size, and the particular cruise itinerary she chose was in an area of the world where the seas could be a bit rough at times.

If your thoughts are similar to the agent's client and the rock and roll of ships makes you shy away from going on a cruise, I would advise you to give it another try. I think you may be pleasantly surprised. **Many technological improvements have taken place in the past 20 years to minimize how much movement ships experience while out at sea, making today's cruise ships head and shoulders above the ones of the past in this regard.** If you decide to cruise again, you might want to consider the following:

- **Make sure your ship has stabilizers.** Nearly all newer cruise ships have them, and they really help provide a smoother ride.
- **Select a large cruise ship.** Although smaller ships provide a more intimate cruising experience, the larger the ship, the more stable it tends to be.
- Go on a cruise in an area of the world and at a time of the year **where the sea is likely to be relatively calm.** For instance, the Caribbean in the spring or the inside passage to Alaska in the summer would probably be safer choices than crossing the Atlantic Ocean would be in the fall.
- Choose a cabin on the ship that is **near the center of the ship** (rather than at the front or the back) and that is **on a lower deck.**

Stabilizers

Stabilizers are an especially useful and helpful invention. Stabilizers are large fins that stick out into the water from each side of the ship. They look a lot like the wings of an airplane. Because a ship is long and narrow, rolling (moving from side to side) is the motion you will notice the most in heavy seas. The rolling of the hull, caused by wave motion, can be greatly reduced by imposing an opposite motion using a stabilizing fin on each side of the ship.

These stabilizing fins are retractable, being stored inside the hull of the ship when the seas are calm or when the ship is docking. If the seas become rough, underwater doors open and the fins are extended. When extended, they operate automatically under the command of a gyroscope located inside the ship. The gyroscope detects the rolling motion of the ship and then sends signals to the stabilizers so that they can adjust to the motion. **The fins create an opposite force to the waves, thereby helping keep the ship from rolling back and forth as much.**

They come in various shapes and sizes so as to match the needs of each ship. As an example, the Star Princess, a ship built in 2002 that carries over 3,100 passengers plus a crew of 1,200, has two stabilizer fins. **Each fin is approximately 25 feet in length, is installed about 15 feet below the water line, and is located nearly halfway between the front and back of the ship.** The gyroscope for the stabilizers is in the engine control room deep down in the hull while the computerized operating panel for the system is high up on the bridge of the ship where the captain and the crew navigate and command the vessel.

Stabilizers, plus other items of modern technology, have greatly improved the cruising experience. **Although no invention can ever totally eliminate all of the rock and roll, I hope that the travel agent's client will give cruising another try.**

Nautical Term

Shanghaied

When someone is shanghaied, he or she is forced or tricked into going somewhere or doing something using deceit or fraud. The word comes from the days when merchant ship owners in California and elsewhere on the west coast often had difficulty finding enough crew members to man their ships. They enlisted agents who were known for using unscrupulous means (such as getting men drunk, making untruthful promises, or even abducting them) to get the men on board ships. By the time the men came to or discovered they had been tricked, it was too late. **The ship had already left port and was on its way to a far-away destination such as Shanghai or some other foreign port. The men had been shanghaied.**

A Light and Whistle on My Life Jacket?

There is a lot more to the life jacket each passenger has in their cabin than meets the eye. Your life jacket, more properly called a **Personal Flotation Device (PFD),** is a modern safety system that must meet many regulations. More technically, **it is a Type I Offshore Life Jacket that meets SOLAS requirements.** SOLAS stands for the International Convention for the Safety of Life at Sea and is an international maritime safety treaty that your cruise ship must adhere to. **In broad terms, SOLAS ensures that ships comply with minimum safety standards in construction, equipment, and operation.** Included in these areas are requirements for life boats, rescue boats, and **life jackets.**

As you take a close look at your life jacket you'll notice that it is bulkier than the ones used on small pleasure boats. **That is because this PFD is designed to work in the open ocean for a long period of time.** It is an inherently buoyant life jacket that provides flotation through the use of closed cell foam. It is rugged, low maintenance, and there is no need to inflate it. It is designed to keep you floating right-side-up in the water for a long time and to assist rescuers in locating you in the water, even if you are injured or are unconscious.

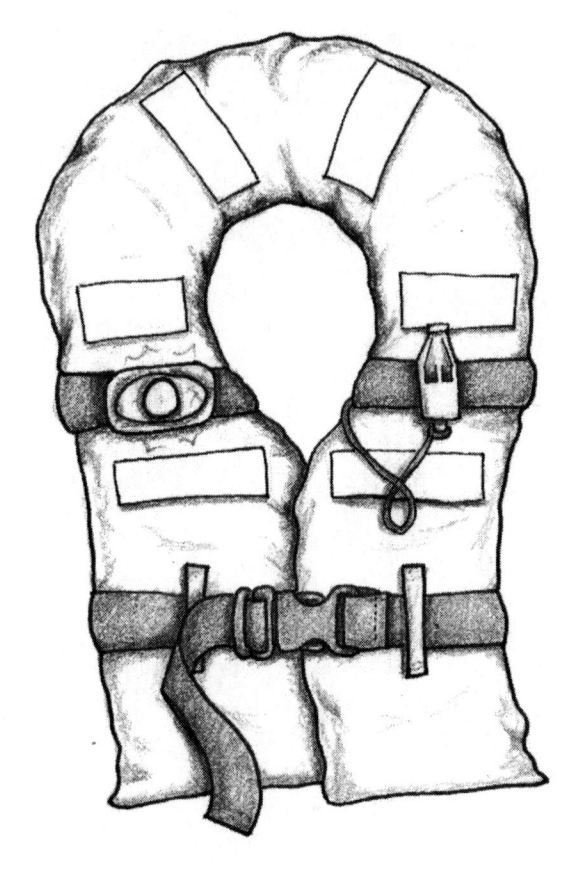

Your bright orange or yellow PFD has an automatic SOLAS-approved light attached to it. The light automatically turns on when it gets wet in both fresh and salt water, provides a bright piercing light that flashes many times each minute, and lasts for more than eight hours at full intensity. You'll also find a **high-pitched whistle** (usually made of plastic) attached to the PFD. The life jacket also has reflective tape sewn onto it so that a search light would readily reflect off it.

And perhaps most importantly, the life jacket has been designed to automatically provide a rotational force that **floats a person to a face-up position** with their body inclined backward to permit proper breathing with their head above the water. Also, it normally has a headrest area and a grab handle to make it easier to pull a person out of the water.

It is interesting to note that it was **soon after the sinking of the Titanic on April 15, 1912** that many new and stricter regulations started to come into being for ships sailing on the oceans. Since that time there has been a steady series of improvements to life jackets, life boats, and other safety equipment to make sure that if there is an emergency on a ship and a passenger ends up in the water, **they will be found and rescued as quickly as possible.**

Nautical Term

Fairway

The word **fairway**, which today we commonly associate with the game of golf, had its origins in the world of ships and seas. **The navigable portion of a harbor or river through which ships entered or left port was known as the fairway.** Likewise, the portion of the golf hole you hope to stay in is called the **fairway.**

Prefabricated Staterooms – Without Floors

The two largest cruise ships ever built, the **Oasis of the Seas** and the **Allure of the Seas**, were built for Royal Caribbean International at a shipyard in **Turku, Finland**. The Oasis entered into service in December 2009 and the Allure in December 2010. With a cost of well over $1 billion per ship, **they hold the distinction of being the most expensive exports to that date ever from the country of Finland.**

About a dozen miles east of the Turku shipyard, nestled in farm country, is a small town called **Piikkiö. While the ships themselves were being constructed in Turku, most of the cabins (Royal Caribbean calls them staterooms) for the ships were being built in Piikkiö by a company located there.** This was being done because prefabricating the staterooms off-site, instead of building them piece-by-piece on the ship, provided significant savings in both time and money.

It is becoming more and more common in the cruise industry for the standard cabins of a ship (as opposed to some large specialty cabins) to be prefabricated off-site and then transported intact to the ship when the ship is ready for them – i.e. when the steel structure for the relevant deck is ready. Large cranes at the shipyard then lift the cabins up to their proper deck where they are carefully fitted into place.

Staterooms

The prefabricated staterooms constructed off-site are usually built without floors – except for the bathroom floors. Once the prefabricated stateroom module is brought to the ship and hoisted to its correct spot, it is anchored to the ship's large steel deck that then serves as the floor of the stateroom. A wide metal band that runs around the bottom of the prefabricated walls is then welded to the metal floor. (Have you noticed these metal bands in any of your staterooms while you have been on a cruise? Sometimes portions of them are visible.) A coat of cement is then spread over the metal floor and finally carpet padding and carpeting is laid down.

Then the utility and service lines (for electrical power, communications, fire safety, water, the vacuum-actuated toilet, etc.), which have already been installed in the prefabricated stateroom and are essentially **plug-in ready,** are connected to the corresponding lines of the ship.

The prefabricated module that is assembled off-site in Piikkiö includes the wall panels, ceiling panels, entry door, and bathroom module -- **as well as all of the things that you find attached and anchored to the walls and ceiling of your** stateroom. These attached items include light fixtures, vanities, desks, wall units, artwork, mirrors, ceiling ventilation units, public address speakers, fire alarms, fire sprinklers, closets, safes, etc. The items not included in the prefabricated stateroom are the things that are movable – sofas, chairs, curtains, beds, bedding, hangers, towels, and the like. The sliding glass door, if the stateroom has a balcony, and the balcony itself are installed after the module has been placed on the ship.

The bathroom, which normally is itself a separately prefabricated unit, is set in place and made part of the stateroom during the off-site assembly process. The bathroom module does have a floor – **typically a hard plastic one that sits several inches higher than what the floor of the stateroom will be.** In the area under this floor are found the water and drain lines that service the wash basin and the shower or bath.

And what if there are problems with the utilities in your stateroom during your cruise? Normally, in the corridor outside your room, there is a locked closet between each set of two staterooms. Inside that closet is where the service areas and utility connections are for each pair of rooms. Repairs usually can be made there instead of having to go into the stateroom to do so. You'll also notice that after every few closets there is a closet with a door that doesn't lock. Inside this closet, in addition to the usual utility connections, you will find fire extinguishing equipment available for both the crew and passengers to use, if needed.

Nautical Term

Under the Weather

If a sailor became too sick to continue with his duties up on the deck of his sailing ship, the captain sent him below deck to get out of the wind, spray, and rain so he could recover. When that happened he was considered to be **under the weather.** That nautical term continues today to describe someone who is feeling ill.

A Stateroom Is Better Than a Cabin – Or Is It?

A friend of mine was quite excited because on their upcoming cruise **they will be in a "stateroom."** On their first cruise several years ago, he said that their accommodations were **"just a cabin."**

What is the difference between a cabin and a stateroom? Is a stateroom better, larger, or fancier than a cabin? Let's consult Webster's Dictionary:

Webster's Definitions
- Cabin – A private room on a ship.
- Stateroom – A private cabin on a ship.

So in the dictionary the two terms are basically interchangeable and even though in today's cruise market the word stateroom is perhaps becoming more popular than the word cabin, there's really no inherent difference in the terms. They're both just a room on a ship.

In the cruise industry, each individual cruise line uses its own terminology for their room accommodations, choosing their array of names in order to better market their products. And there's a lot to choose from! **One ship in today's cruise market may offer as many as a dozen types of cabin/stateroom configurations on the ship – and as many as forty different brochure price categories.**

In general, cruise ships offer **three main types** of accommodations:
- **Suites** – These are the largest living spaces on board and typically have private balconies. Suites are marketed under various names such as grand suite, penthouse, mini-suite, junior suite, garden villa, loft suite, romance suite, verandah suite, etc.
- **Outside View Cabins/Staterooms** – These rooms may have a private balcony (sometimes called a verandah) or they may have a large picture window or one or more round portholes.
- **Interior Cabins/Staterooms** – These accommodations do not have a window or a porthole – no outside source of light.

STATEROOM   CABIN

The price you pay for a cabin/stateroom is related to a number of factors, including:
- **Size** – The more square footage, the higher the price. Brochures usually indicate the square footage and show a layout of the room. And it is amazing what a range of sizes are available on today's ships – from as small as **90 square feet to as much as 4,390 square feet!**

- **Location** – Generally, the higher the deck, the higher the room's price and the better the service. And many feel that cabins/staterooms near the center of the ship may be more stable in rough seas and more isolated from noise and vibrations than ones fore and aft.
- **Facilities** – What is offered inside the room also influences the price. High-grade cabins/staterooms, and especially suites, may have full-size bathtubs, queen beds, separate vanities, larger TVs, and more spacious closets and drawers. On the lower end of the price scale will be smaller beds, berths rather than beds, walk-in showers, tighter spaces, etc.

So which is better? A cabin or a stateroom? Since the terminology usually means about the same thing, you'll need to study and compare the various accommodation choices available on the ship each time you book a cruise and not make the decision solely on what names the cruise line gives their rooms.

And, by the way, it turns out that my friend's "stateroom" on their next trip **is actually 20 square feet smaller** than the "cabin" they were in on their first cruise.

Nautical Term

Aloof

Aloof: As in "to keep a distance from, to be apart from." Sailing ship captains were expected to make the fastest time they could from their port of origin to their destination. This required positioning their ship at all times to take full advantage of the wind. Originally a nautical order to keep the ship's head to the wind, **aloof means to sail close to the wind and to stay clear of and to keep a distance from the lee-shore or leeward where the winds are not to the ship's advantage.**

Ft. Lauderdale, We Have a Problem. A Good One!

Ft. Lauderdale, we have a problem. A good one! The cruise ship terminal in Ft. Lauderdale, Florida (known as Port Everglades) is the embarkation and disembarkation point for two ships that have created a bit of an interesting problem for their passengers. The Oasis of the Seas and the Allure of the Seas advertise that **there are 25 possible ways to dine on board each ship.**

Both of these ships, the largest ones currently in service, sail 7-night Eastern and 7-night Western Caribbean itineraries. Allure sails from Port Everglades each Sunday afternoon and returns on Sunday morning a week later. Oasis does the same thing on Saturdays. **The problem? Well, let's do the math.** A 7-night cruise provides 21 meal times (two on the first day, three on each of the next six days, and one on the last day). So, unless the passengers choose to eat more than three meals per day on several of the days, they can't try all of the possible ways to dine. There is not enough time. And to make matters worse, each itinerary includes three port calls, so there are three days where lunch will probably be eaten off the ship. **So now we are down** to just **18 meal times and 25 options during the cruise.** Now that's a good problem to have!

These two large ships help illustrate how **the food part of cruising has changed over the years.** Among the many changes that have taken place, here are several of the significant ones:

Greater Selection – Passengers have a much greater selection of eating venues available to them than in the past, at least on the larger cruise ships. **Besides the regular dining room and buffet, more and more ships have a variety of specialty restaurants and eateries to choose from (many of them at an extra cost).** For instance, on the Allure of the Seas there is an exclusive high-end restaurant, a Brazilian steak house, an Italian trattoria, a Mexican cantina, an Asian restaurant, a chop house, a pizzeria, a bistro, a hamburger diner, a hot dog place, a donut shop, an ice cream parlor, a health food bar in the spa – and, of course, there are also midnight buffets, chocolate buffets, the main dining room, and room service.

Up-to-You Flexible Dining – For many years, passengers on cruises have been assigned a certain time and a certain table to eat at in the dining rooms. Today, most cruise ships continue to offer fixed-time dining, but more and more ships are also including up-to-you flexible dining. **Passengers may show up whenever they wish during the hours the main dining rooms**

are open and they do not have to sit at a pre-assigned table with a pre-assigned group. They are welcome to eat just by themselves if a table is available, or they may join with other passengers for the meal.

Greater Care in Food Preparation – Cruise lines, as well as government health officials, are extremely concerned about illnesses and outbreaks of diseases during cruises. When it comes to food, the regulations pertaining to the storing, preparing, and serving of food are **much more stringent than in the past.** If you have ever gone on a recent galley tour of a ship, you will have noticed the spotless stainless steel kitchens and heard about the numerous rules that govern the handling of food. These rules are much more detailed and comprehensive now than in the past.

Healthier Foods – Despite the great quantities of food available everywhere and at all times on cruises, **it is getting easier and easier to eat healthy meals.** Most menus on board point out the low-calorie and health-conscious choices, and many ships now have cafes and eateries dedicated solely to healthy eating.

Orson Welles said, **"Ask not what you can do for your country. Ask what's for lunch."** If you subscribe to this kind of thinking and if food is a big part of the reason you like to cruise, then you are in luck. Your problem on one of today's mega-cruise ships will be a good one to have – **the wonderful problem of deciding which of all the eating options on board the ship to choose next.**

Nautical Term

Slush Fund

A slush fund is an unregulated and auxiliary reserve fund of money. The term was originally associated with ships and sailors. **The slush was the fat or grease that was left over from boiling salted meat.** When the ship arrived in port, the slush could be sold to candle makers or tanneries on shore and the money obtained from the sale could then be used **to provide the crew with extra luxuries – thus they had a slush fund.**

The Road Less Traveled

One of the nice aspects of cruising is that there are many different ways for passengers to spend their time while their ship is in port for the day. One of my own favorite days on shore was in the **Falkland Islands** while my wife and I were on a cruise that took us around the southern tip of South America. The experience I had there reminded me of Robert Frost's poem, *The Road Not Taken*. Concerning the two roads that diverged in a yellow wood, he wrote,

> **"I took the one less traveled by,
> and that made all the difference."**

Before we left on our cruise, we carefully went over the various shore excursions offered by the cruise line in each port of call on the trip. There were eight stops on the itinerary. **A total of 54 possible shore excursions were offered** – an average of nearly seven per port. The prices of the shore excursions ranged from **$27 per person on the low end** (a short city tour in Montevideo, Uruguay) **to $2,999 per person on the high end** (an airplane flight to Antarctica for a day's visit to a research station there). After reviewing what was available, we signed up for a number of shore excursions before we left home. However, when it came to our stop in the Falkland Islands, we decided to keep our morning there open and to just do something on our own.

Upon going ashore in Port Stanley, the capital city of the Falkland Islands, we split up. **My wife looked around the quaint village and went shopping (her favorite thing to do), while I decided to see if the golf course (my favorite thing to do) that had been built by British soldiers in the 1930s was still there.**

Not knowing where to go, I found an elderly local man on the dock and asked him about the golf course. He looked to me to be an honest and safe person and he invited me to get into his car and proceeded to give me a lift to the course, which was a little ways outside of the city. He chuckled when I told him I wanted to play golf there, and when we arrived at the course after driving down a bumpy rural road, I understood why he laughed. What once was a nice golf course built on the side of a beautiful hill overlooking the South Atlantic Ocean was now a nearly-abandoned site with **overgrown fairways and, shall we say, some interesting greens.**

Whenever I travel, I take with me a small cloth bag with several golf balls, some tees, some golf ball markers, and a golf glove. I then rent clubs at the course where I want to play. Well, this course's pro shop was a little brown wooden building with all of the doors and windows locked. Cut into one of the exterior walls was a small slot. Next to the slot was a sign that said, **"Honesty Box."** This was apparently where you were to pay for using the course. I was about to give up on playing golf there when I noticed **several old golf clubs lying in the grass** a few feet to the side of the club house. Not seeing anyone around, and with my ride having already returned to Port Stanley, I slid some money into the Honesty Box slot and decided to give the course a try.

Several hours later I was glad that I had chosen **the road less traveled** during our visit to the Falkland Islands. **My quirky round of golf there had been wonderful!** By trial and error I had discovered that the course had 18 tees but only 12 greens. Six of the greens were used twice. The weather during my round had been pleasant, the scenery spectacular, and I was able to play as many balls as I wanted without worrying about holding up anyone else on the course – because there was no one else in sight. And I shot one of my lowest scores ever. (Of course, I only counted the very best of all of the balls I played on each hole and I was not above moving my ball if the lie wasn't real good.)

As I left the course and took a leisurely stroll back to town, I was smiling. I never would have imagined that I would play golf in the Falkland Islands. Even today, just thinking about it makes me chuckle. As I got back to town I had some fish and chips in a charming local pub and then met up with my wife for our afternoon shore excursion to visit some battlefields.

I am grateful that on that beautiful morning in the Falkland Islands I took **the road less traveled – a road that made all the difference on that day.**

Nautical Term

Loose Lips Sink Ships

This phrase is of fairly recent origin. **During World War II, servicemen and civilians were cautioned by the US Office of War Information to be discreet in their talk to avoid leaking information to the enemy.** People were especially warned not to reveal the location of a Navy ship on which a loved one was serving so that the enemy would not know about US ship movements. Today the phrase **"Loose Lips Sink Ships"** is still used to indicate that we should avoid careless and unguarded talk – because you never know who might be listening and you never know what damage your words might cause.

I Love Teak Deck Chairs!

My first experiences with **teak deck chairs and teak deck lounges (also called steamer chairs)** were as a young boy crossing the Atlantic, first on the Nieuw Amsterdam and several years later on the Queen Mary (the ship that is now a hotel in Long Beach harbor.) Early each morning on those voyages my parents would hurry up on deck to stake claim to several of those beautiful-looking and pleasant-smelling pieces of furniture. We would then spend a good portion of the day napping, reading, playing shuffleboard, snacking, sunning, and visiting as we relaxed on those chairs that were our home away from our cabin.

Even now when I cruise, I prefer the wooden type of lounge chair to a plastic one if I can find one on a sun deck or in a pool area. **Because teak has become rather scarce and is very expensive -- and because it is a flammable material, true teak furniture on cruise ships is becoming less common.** Other less expensive and safer materials (safer from a fire regulation standpoint) have taken over.

A teak tree is a tropical hardwood tree of the birch family. It is native to Southeast Asia but is also cultivated in other areas of the world. Reaching as high as 150 feet, its wood is yellowish-brown with a strong grain and texture. It is easily worked but can readily blunt saws and knives because there is silica (sand) in the wood. Teak resin contains a natural oil that makes the wood resistant to termites and pests. The oil is also highly water resistant, making teak ideal for outdoor furniture, boat decks, cutting boards, etc.

Teak has a distinctive aroma that now is often associated with ships. Teak furniture holds its form over many years, even when left outside in the elements. It doesn't become brittle and doesn't need preservatives – although occasional polishing or varnishing helps enhance its natural beauty.

So when you do have the privilege of being on a cruise ship that has beautiful teak deck chairs and deck lounges, I hope you appreciate them. Even though trying to figure out how to fold and unfold them can be a trial, in my opinion they are an important part of the cruise experience.

And in case you might want one for yourself for your deck or patio at home, you'll find a number of manufacturers who would be happy to sell you one – but be aware that they are not cheap.

Nautical Term

Skyscraper

Today's extra-tall buildings are, of course, referred to as **skyscrapers**. This term derives its origin from **sailing ships**. During times when the wind was unusually light, a sailing vessel would often raise **a lightweight triangular-shaped sail called a skyscraper** high above the other sails in order to catch every breath of wind available.

What About Cruise Ship Art Auctions?

Cruise ships have a number of ways of earning additional income from their passengers. Through spas, casinos, art auctions, jewelry shops, photography, clothing stores, and shore excursions they bring in additional revenue, revenue that is important to their bottom line. **One of these extra income sources, the art auction, has met with some controversy over the years.** In fact, there have been lawsuits over art sales and art auctions on cruise ships.

The cruise ships that have fine artwork for sale normally have the art on display in an art gallery as well as in certain high-traffic corridors and lounges of the ship. **Passengers may purchase the artwork from the vendor at an agreed-upon price or they may bid for it at one of the art auctions held periodically on the ship.** As an inducement to attend the auction, the vendor often provides free champagne to those who come. The art company then packages the art that is sold and ships it to the passengers after the cruise, unless the passengers want to take it home with them.

In most cases, the art company is a concessionaire who pays the cruise line a percentage of the sales they achieve. That is, the cruise ship allows a private art vendor to bring the art onboard the ship and then the vendor sells it to the passengers. For allowing the vendor to do so, the cruise ship receives a portion of the sales receipts. (Please note, however, that there is at least one major cruise company that does all of their art sales and auctions themselves rather than using an outside vendor.)

The complaints and lawsuits dealing with art auctions have generally focused on three types of things: **the business** practices of the auction company, the authenticity of the artwork as represented by the auction company, and the prices charged for the artwork. Without making a judgment as to the validity of the complaints and the lawsuits, perhaps I might suggest a few ideas to keep in mind if you are considering purchasing artwork on ships:

- **It is Your Vacation** – A cruise is your vacation. **How you spend your time and your money on it is totally up to you.** You don't have any obligation to do anything you don't want to do, to buy anything you don't want to buy, or to attend anything you don't want to attend. All of that really goes without saying, but it is interesting to see how often people on vacation succumb to promotions and pressure and end up buying things they later regret that they bought.
- **Buyer Beware** – Especially while traveling, keep in mind the importance of the phrase **"buyer beware."** While you may be an expert on the values of goods and services in your own area, you need to be cautious when buying things when away from home.
- **US Laws May Not Apply** - US consumer protection laws do not apply when you are not in the US. **Art auctions are normally conducted while the ship is out at sea** and therefore may not be covered by any US laws.
- **Sales are Final** – Because art sales on ships are final, there usually is little or no recourse after the sale.
- **Investment Quality Items** - Be especially careful when buying things such as artwork that are promoted to you as being of investment quality. **Before entering into any kind of an investment, you would normally want to do proper due diligence concerning it – to carefully check it out.** This can be very difficult to do on artwork, especially while you are on a cruise.
- **Large-Ticket Items** - **Be cautious when purchasing large-ticket items when you are away from home.** If you get taken on a small item when traveling, that is

kind of part of the adventure of going abroad. But none of us likes to be duped when a lot of money is at stake.

Personally, I like to think of the art sales and auctions on ships as an interesting form of ship-board entertainment. I don't take them too seriously. If I see something I like at a price I am comfortable with, I might buy it. Otherwise I let it go.

I hope you have fun on your cruise – on every part of it. I hope that everything you do and all that you buy, including perhaps artwork, will bring you satisfaction, enjoyment, and no regrets. When you return home I hope you feel that your money has been well spent and that you can't wait until your next cruise.

Nautical Term

Founder ... Or Is It Flounder?

Two words that can be easily mixed up are **founder** and **flounder**. **Founder** (from the Latin word meaning bottom, as in foundation) **means to sink, to become submerged, or to become disabled.** Founder is a nautical term associated with ships. When a ship is foundering it needs help ASAP. It is probably sinking.

Flounder, on the other hand, means to thrash about wildly or helplessly -- or to be in a state of confusion.

About the Author

Born in Salt Lake City, Utah, Lee H. Van Dam has also lived in The Netherlands and Hong Kong. He holds an MBA degree and is the owner of a real estate management, sales, and consulting firm.

Lee and his wife, Holly, are the parents of two children and have seven grandchildren. They love to travel and, even though they live many miles from the nearest cruise ship port, they especially enjoy cruising.